S0-DLE-011

You didn't have to give away a portion of your assets, but you did.

Left unanswered in all the necessary legal documents is a simple, but profound question:

why?

What motivated you to make that choice?

What values are implied in your philanthropy and where did they come from?

What are your deepest dreams and hopes for making a difference?

Those you have entrusted to honor your true intentions would really love to know.

Take 5 steps to create an expression of your intent.

Expressions of Donor Intent

What is an expression of donor intent?

It is a letter or recording created to share your motivations, hopes and goals with heirs, successor trustees and/or beneficiaries of your philanthropy in a direct, personal and enduring way.

What are the benefits of creating one?

You ensure that your goals are completely understood, providing the foundation for a spirit of common purpose and harmony among your successors, rather than conflict and division. You will create a repository of memory and values that will touch and guide all those who follow you.

How is it different from a mission statement?

A mission statement defines the kinds of gifts you want to make – where and how – including the issues, populations served or geographic focus. However, in what is usually a few brief lines, by itself a mission statement cannot capture the fullness of your life and the breadth of your intent, so valuable for successors to hear directly from you.

Is it a legal document?

No, it is a strictly personal message, a non-binding complement to legal documents. It is very important that nothing in your expression of intent clouds or contradicts your legal documents. It is advisable to review with your attorney the language of all relevant documents, both binding and non-binding, to ensure that your true intentions will be carried out.

What should not be included?

Words are powerful. These will last forever, so keep a positive tone and focus on what would be helpful for your successors to know, always staying true to the terms of your governance documents.

Where should it be kept?

Once it is finished, it should be signed, dated and kept with related legal documents, updated as necessary. You might want to consider sharing it while you are alive, and enjoy the benefits of the conversations that will follow.

Message from the Authors

We created this guidebook because the legal documents establishing charitable instruments simply do not reflect the richness of personal history, values and visions that lie behind the giving. Our experience has proven to us that this information is just too valuable – for donors, families and recipients – not to capture and preserve, for all those who are:

- Setting up a philanthropic foundation or fund
- Trying to discern the intent of a deceased donor, or
- Designating a charitable bequest in an estate plan

Each charitable path is unique, and it is our goal to provide a means for self-expression in a process that is orderly, adaptable and personally rewarding.

As you go through the questions and exercises on the following pages – alone or as a couple or group – use the space provided to record brief notes for yourself. You will be using these notes as reference in the final step of the process to create your enduring expression of intent.

Whether you ultimately chose to express yourself in writing or on an audio or video recording, what you create will be a profound and timeless gift, both in your lifetime and beyond.

May you enjoy every step!

SUSAN TURNBULL
Personal Legacy Advisors

AMY ZELL ELLSWORTH
The Philanthropic Initiative

The 5 Steps

For Your Readers

? ASK YOURSELF: Who will be responsible for carrying out your intent in the future?

CHECK ALL THAT APPLY:

- ❏ Children
- ❏ Grandchildren
- ❏ Great grandchildren and beyond
- ❏ Spouse
- ❏ Other family member(s)
- ❏ Non-family successor trustee(s) known to you

- ❏ Non-family successor trustee(s) unknown to you
- ❏ Institution for which the gift is intended
- ❏ _____
- ❏ _____
- ❏ _____

? ASK YOURSELF: What do you hope to achieve with this document?

CHECK ALL THAT APPLY:

- ❏ Explain your charitable motivations
- ❏ Articulate your charitable priorities
- ❏ Provide information otherwise not known
- ❏ Transmit your values
- ❏ Share some family history
- ❏ Share some personal history

- ❏ Affirm your love for those you are addressing
- ❏ Personalize the legal documents
- ❏ Preserve your 'voice' over time
- ❏ _____
- ❏ _____
- ❏ _____

To our descendants,

It has given us the greatest pride and pleasure to establish the Wilcox Foundation. The legal documents lay out what we hope is a good system for sharing leadership, and include a mission statement we feel is flexible enough to address future challenges we cannot predict. What the legal document fails to do, however, is to capture the spirit behind our decision to create this charitable foundation, a spirit we dream of keeping alive for many generations of our family. There are a few things we want you each to know about why we did what we did, and the kind of positive impact we hope this will have on all of you, and on the larger world.

FOR EXAMPLE:

Moretti Family Foundation

Friedman Environmental Trust

The Amiri Family Donor Advised Fund (at the local community foundation)

Wei Institute for Advanced Study (at the State University)

Charles and Elizabeth Stratton Scholarship Fund

Gift to the Childhood Diabetes Research Institute

EXAMPLES OF SALUTATIONS:

To my dearest descendants

To the King County Community Foundation

To the successor trustees of Richland Trust

To the recipients of the Smith Family Scholarships

Dear Mary, Ted and Rose

YOUR NAME:

NAME OF CHARITABLE FOUNDATION, FUND OR GIFT:

If you know the names of those to whom your expression of intent will be written, write down their names and create a salutation.

DEAR

If their names are not known to you, write a general salutation to those you will be addressing.

TO

Personal and Philanthropic Values

Personal values may not always be easy to articulate, but they lie at the core of who you are and what is important to you, including your decision to give. Values are born of experience and defining personal influences, and are manifested every day in the way you live your life.

The following several pages ask you consider these values. You will have the chance to think about how to express those values to your audience naturally, through stories. In this way, you reinforce your living example and open a door for your successors to understand how you became the person – and the donor – that you are.

Using the values list on the opposite page as a helpful reference, let the questions in Step Two trigger your memories and thoughts about what inspires and drives you at the deepest level.

If you are in the position of a successor trying to identify the values of someone who is no longer alive, try to put yourselves in their shoes and answer the questions from their point of view as best you can.

One of my earliest memories from childhood is from the weekends before Christmas. Each year, my father would bundle us into the car for a ride to the small factory where he worked in downtown Buffalo. There we would pick up baskets that contained everything for a holiday dinner plus decorations and a small gift or two. We would drive from the factory to a neighborhood with multi-family houses packed close together and deliver the baskets. I remember understanding that without our delivery, these families would have a cold Christmas indeed. The delight on their faces and the pleasure of bringing something valuable into their lives has always stayed with me.

Values List *(Add any others that you wish)*

❑ Beauty	❑ Heritage	❑ Pride
❑ Change	❑ Honesty	❑ Privacy
❑ Choice	❑ Hope	❑ Proficiency
❑ Citizenship	❑ Humility	❑ Prudence
❑ Collaboration	❑ Humor	❑ Respect
❑ Commitment	❑ Idealism	❑ Responsibility
❑ Community	❑ Independence	❑ Resourcefulness
❑ Compassion	❑ Individuality	❑ Security
❑ Competition	❑ Innocence	❑ Self-discipline
❑ Confidence	❑ Innovation	❑ Self-expression
❑ Courage	❑ Intelligence	❑ Self-reliance
❑ Creativity	❑ Integrity	❑ Self-respect
❑ Dignity	❑ Interdependence	❑ Service
❑ Diversity	❑ Joy	❑ Serenity
❑ Education	❑ Justice	❑ Simplicity
❑ Empathy	❑ Kindness	❑ Spirituality
❑ Enthusiasm	❑ Knowledge	❑ Sportsmanship
❑ Entrepreneurship	❑ Leadership	❑ Stewardship
❑ Equality	❑ Love	❑ Success
❑ Excellence	❑ Loyalty	❑ Thrift
❑ Fairness	❑ Merit	❑ Tolerance
❑ Faith	❑ Modesty	❑ Tradition
❑ Family	❑ Nature	❑ Truth
❑ Freedom	❑ Opportunity	❑ Wealth
❑ Forgiveness	❑ Optimism	❑ Wisdom
❑ Generosity	❑ Order	❑ _____
❑ Gratitude	❑ Patience	❑ _____
❑ Happiness	❑ Patriotism	❑ _____
❑ Harmony	❑ Peace	❑ _____
❑ Health	❑ Perseverance	

Personal and Philanthropic Values

? ASK YOURSELF: What two or three experiences stand out as having had a pivotal impact on your life?

✱ WHAT VALUES DO YOU ASSOCIATE WITH THESE EXPERIENCES?

? ASK YOURSELF: What are two or three things that you learned from your parents and/or grandparents?

✱ WHAT POSITIVE VALUES DID THEY MODEL?

I grew up hearing stories of my great grandparents' lives during the Depression. They owned a grocery store in one of the poorer neighborhoods of St. Paul. Often their clients had difficulty paying their bills, but my grandfather was always ready to extend credit. He would slice up a salami to give to adults and always had a treat for the children when they came to the store. In addition, my grandmother had a reputation for providing a hot meal for people who came to the back door…along with some chores for them to do acknowledging what they had to offer as well. In their turn, my parents continued their own form of giving and sharing. I remember one autumn driving down the street with my mother on the way home from school. We passed a woman on the street who clearly was not dressed for the changing weather. My mother pulled to the side of the street and engaged the woman in conversation. By the time they parted, the woman was wearing my mother's coat.

? **ASK YOURSELF:** What activities and roles are high priorities in your life now?

WHAT VALUES ARE EXPRESSED IN THESE PRIORITIES?

? **ASK YOURSELF:** What personal and family stories come to mind from the previous questions? Which ones are important for your successors to know? Which ones would you enjoy relating? Hearing stories about your deepest influences will help them see the world through your eyes.

STORIES OF WHICH YOU ARE REMINDED:

Motivations for Your Giving

People give for many reasons based on their upbringing, their life experience and their personal values. Consider what has motivated your altruism so you can share that inspiration with those who will continue the work after you.

? **ASK YOURSELF:** Look over the list below. Check the top factors that motivate you to give and set aside funds for future giving.

❏ You find joy in helping others

❏ You feel it is the right thing to do

❏ It is a way to express your gratitude

❏ It has financial/estate planning advantages

❏ It is something your parents did

❏ Your spiritual traditions suggest it

❏ You are following the example of someone you admire

❏ You would like to help solve a specific problem

❏ _____

❏ _____

❏ _____

I grew up pretty poor in the Bronx and while you can take the boy out of the old neighborhood, you can't ever take the neighborhood out of the boy. I spent far more time trying to earn money than studying, and while not proud of that, early on realized I could sell almost anything – plus I loved it. So when the business began to really grow it was the most natural thing in the world to give back. You never forget where you are from, and the foundation I established is the best kind of legacy. From where I started it is still amazing I ended up in this position.

For each motivating factor you checked, there is very likely a story behind it – about a person, an experience or a situation. Consider which stories would help your successors understand your history and point of view.

STORIES OF WHICH YOU ARE REMINDED:

 WHAT VALUES DO YOU ASSOCIATE WITH THESE STORIES?

? **ASK YOURSELF:** How do you hope you will be remembered?

 WHAT VALUES ARE EXPRESSED IN YOUR RESPONSE?

The History of Your Giving

What does your giving history say about what you feel is most important? How does it contribute to your vision for the future? Will you want your successors to focus on the areas of greatest interest to you? Or do you want them to discover for themselves the greatest needs and interests when they become trustees or advisors to your foundation or fund?

? **ASK YOURSELF:** What have been some of your most important and meaningful gifts?

As a young man, I always wanted to go to college. Circumstances prevented me from having that privilege, but I have met many young people, starting with the young men who worked in my business, whom I've been able to both encourage and support to go on in school. I think the most exciting thing to me has been the combination of helping pay for scholarships and mentoring young people through their years in college. It has always seemed a way to carry out my deepest feelings about hope, equality, opportunity and generosity.

? **ASK YOURSELF:** Each gift listed on the previous page has a story behind it. Which gifts are most meaningful and why? Pick a few and consider the stories you would enjoy sharing with your successors.

STORIES OF WHICH YOU ARE REMINDED:

? **ASK YOURSELF:** What do I want my successors to do? *Check to make sure.*

❏ I would prefer that they continue to give primarily in my areas of interest

❏ I want them to feel completely free to choose their own areas of interest

❏ Marked on the spectrum below is the balance I want them to achieve between my priorities and theirs

I____O____O____O____O____O____I
Mine   *Theirs*

Note: Do your governance documents reflect your preference?

? **ASK YOURSELF:** Consider the way you marked the spectrum above. Why is that your preference? Explain below.

✳ BOTH DURING AND AFTER MY LIFE, THE VALUES I WISH TO PROMOTE AND ENCOURAGE WITH MY GIVING ARE:

The Values Behind the Assets

The financial assets that anchor your giving are like the proverbial "tip of the iceberg." Unless shared, all that lies beneath the surface – the multidimensional story of the creation of the wealth – will be lost in the space of a generation. It is too interesting, and too valuable, not to share with your successors and help establish a foundation for healthy and realistic values about money.

? **ASK YOURSELF:** Where did the money come from?

CHECK ALL THAT APPLY, MINDFUL THAT SOME MAY OVERLAP:

❑ Employment earnings

❑ Stock option grants or restricted shares

❑ Family business

❑ Your own business or enterprise

❑ Physical assets: real estate, art, mineral rights, etc.

❑ Financial assets: stocks, bonds, etc.

❑ Inheritance

❑ Gifts

❑ Trust or annuity

❑ Life insurance proceeds

❑ Windfall: lottery, lawsuit, etc.

❑ _____

❑ _____

❑ _____

❑ _____

You know the basic story of how our business began, but less familiar to you, and certainly unknown by your children, is the story of my grandfather's life and his legacy to me – not only in terms of his personal example, but the assets I inherited from him. This handful of stocks grew over time to provide some of the seed capital for our business, which in turn enabled creation of the foundation. The foundation cannot be separated from the story, a story I want to preserve.

? ASK YOURSELF: For each source you checked on the opposite page, there is yet another layer of stories and driving values – of ideas, people, struggles and achievements. Which of those stories should be preserved for your successors? Which would you enjoy telling? What are the life lessons that emerge? What are the values that shine through the stories?

STORIES OF WHICH YOU ARE REMINDED:

WHAT VALUES DO YOU ASSOCIATE WITH THESE STORIES?

WRITING YOUR OWN CHAPTER

I will feel I have created a positive legacy with my financial assets when these outcomes are achieved:

When people remember me and my approach toward the use of my financial resources, I hope they will
say that I was:

A Vision for Your Philanthropy

A vision is a mental picture of what you hope to accomplish. When it is articulated it can provide inspiration and clarity to your successors as they ask themselves, "Does this action contribute to the realization of the vision?"

? **ASK YOURSELF:** Do you already have a mission and/or vision statement?
(A mission statement succinctly articulates the purpose of the philanthropy. A vision statement is an image of the philanthropy's mission accomplished.)

If so, write it/them here:

? **ASK YOURSELF:** Is this vision and/or mission statement an accurate reflection of your purpose? If not, what language needs to be changed?

(If you do not have a vision and/or mission statement, you may want to create them to incorporate into your governance documents. Use this longer expression of intent as the vehicle to explain yourself more fully to your successors, giving them a well-rounded picture of your reasoning, goals and hopes.)

We imagine you coming together on a regular basis to talk about what you most care about and to make gifts together based on a shared understanding. We envision you discussing and even debating what is most important for society and allowing your gifts to reflect your shared values. We care about this because we feel the best way to stay close as a family is to understand what is important to each other and to be engaged in an enterprise that is larger than family – that looks beyond day to day concerns.

Our interests have run the gamut from arts and culture to parenting education. However, we have always thought about the needs of young children and hope that you will focus much of your attention and gifts to benefit children ages 0 – 10 years of age. These early years are the ones that have the most impact on a person's life. It is the time for instilling an eagerness to learn and engage the world – and we remember what it was like to see your understanding and lives unfold during those years.

Your philanthropic venture will no doubt have an impact on many people. If inclusion of your family is a high priority for you, your vision of impact will include both them and society. You may feel that a shared family endeavor is what is most important to you. On the other hand, you may feel the highest goal is to carry out specific philanthropic goals for society. There is no right or wrong answer, but giving direction to successors will avoid wrangling and heartache in the future.

ASK YOURSELF: Broadly speaking, what is your vision for having a positive impact with your philanthropy? On the spectrum below, indicate the relative importance of family and society to your vision. Which is more important to you? Is it more of one than the other or an equal balance?

| _____O_____O_____O_____O_____O_____ |

Sustaining family relationships and values   *Alleviating unmet needs of society*

ASK YOURSELF: Imagine a newspaper story 20 years from now announcing an event to honor your philanthropy. What would the headline read?

ASK YOURSELF: Imagine your successors working together in philanthropy 20 years from now. Who is involved? How are they communicating and making decisions? What is the most important reason they are together? What is the one thing you hope they will never lose sight of?

For Your Family

ASK YOURSELF: What is your vision of what the philanthropy will bring to your family?

# YOUR PRIORITIES	YOU HOPE THAT YOUR FAMILY WILL
	Learn to make decisions and work together
	Get to know each other in deep and significant ways
	Learn about and understand the needs of society
	Carry on the values of family and a philanthropic legacy
	Build skills for the next and future generations
	Discover for themselves what they most care about
	Use these resources to support causes they care about
	Be personally inspired by your example

ASK YOURSELF: For each of your top three priorities above, jot down notes explaining why it's important to you.

PRIORITY #1 This is important to you because

PRIORITY #2 This is important to you because

PRIORITY #3 This is important to you because

STEP 3:   CONTEMPLATE YOUR VISION

For Society

? **ASK YOURSELF:** How do you want to have an impact in society?

# YOUR PRIORITIES	YOU HOPE THE PHILANTHROPY WILL
	Make a difference for the issues you care most about
	Support the organizations you care most about
	Support the community where you live
	Support the community where the wealth was created
	Make a difference globally
	Make the greatest difference/have the greatest impact
	Help those in greatest need

? **ASK YOURSELF:** How do you want to have an impact in society?

PRIORITY #1 This is important to you because

PRIORITY #2 This is important to you because

PRIORITY #3 This is important to you because

www.tpi.org & www.personallegacyadvisors.com   **19**

A Reflection of Your Intent

How do your governance documents reflect your values and vision? This section allows you to share your thoughts about the provisions of any legal documents that exist for your philanthropic instrument. In preparation, you may want review them to ensure they are in order and that they adequately reflect and support your intent.

? ASK YOURSELF: What exists already?

CHECK ALL THAT APPLY

❏ Vision statement
❏ Mission statement
❏ Articles of organization
❏ Bylaws
❏ Fund agreement
❏ Trust instrument

❏ Letters of agreement with recipients
❏ Other governance documents
❏ _____
❏ _____
❏ _____

? ASK YOURSELF: Do you have preferences that are not already documented that you would like to express to your successors?

NOTE THEM BELOW

GIFT RESTRICTIONS: Are there particular organizations to support or exclude?

_____
_____
_____
_____

TYPES OF GIFTS ALLOWED:
❏ General operating support
❏ Project support
❏ Endowment
❏ Capital projects
❏ _____
❏ _____
❏ _____

SUCCESSOR TRUSTEES/ADVISORS: Are there particular criteria or conditions for new trustees or advisors?

❏ Family member
❏ Age
❏ Interest
❏ Experience
❏ Skills
❏ _____
❏ _____
❏ _____

PERPETUITY OR SUNSET:

❏ You imagine the fund/foundation existing in perpetuity
❏ There is a sunset clause
❏ Each succeeding generation will make the decision about sunsetting

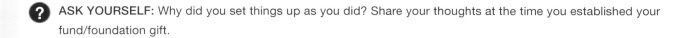

? **ASK YOURSELF:** Why did you set things up as you did? Share your thoughts at the time you established your fund/foundation gift.

? **ASK YOURSELF:** Are there provisions or preferences that are particularly important? List them and explain why they are important.

When we sold our business in 1990, we were advised by our accountant that for tax reasons we might want to establish a charitable foundation. We didn't think about it a lot at the time, and so our documents are fairly "boiler plate." However, it has subsequently given us enormous pleasure to share our good fortune with others and to try to make a difference for others.

Your Outline

You have completed the brainstorming steps of this process. Take a few minutes now to go back through the pages and read through all the notes you have made. Begin to sift these notes, deciding which stories, thoughts and information get at the essence of what you want your successors to understand about you and what you hope to accomplish. Transfer your key notes into the spaces below to create an outline.

A word of advice: At the start, imagine how long you would like the document or recording to be and plan accordingly. Focus your attention on a few key points, knowing you can always add to it later.

 ASK YOURSELF: Knowing it is impossible to tell every story and share every thought, what has emerged in the brainstorming process as being most important to share with your successors?

SALUTATION

Dear/to:

OPENING LINES

The reasons why you wish to create this document

YOUR VALUES

The values that shaped you

The factors that motivated your giving

Your giving history and preferences for the future

YOUR VALUES *(continued)*

The history and values behind the assets that support this gift

YOUR VISION

Your vision for positive impact on the family

Your vision for positive impact on society

THE GOVERNANCE DOCUMENTS

Your original intention

Provisions that need explanation

Preferences that are not spelled out in the governance document

Disclaimer: It is very important that your expression of intent does not cloud or contradict your governance documents. Your expression of intent should include this disclaimer: *To the extent that there is any conflict between my expression of intent and the instrument's governance documents, the legal document shall take precedence.*

CLOSING THOUGHTS

Expression of Intent

You have done a lot of thinking about what you want to say and you have created a structure to follow. With this thoughtful preparatory work behind you, you are ready to create your expression of donor intent in a medium that feels comfortable to you – paper, computer, audio or video recording.

Start by expressing what is easiest to talk about, even if that means starting in the middle of your outline. Move out from there, remembering to relax and be yourself.

New thoughts may come to you in the process. As these new insights merge with the elements you identified in the pages of this guide, your document/recording will take shape. If you speak from the heart, you will not go wrong.

Once you are finished, sign and date your document. In the case of a recording, state your name and date, and then have a printed transcript made so your thoughts will be preserved even with changing technology.

Send a copy to your attorney, file it with the relevant legal documents, and revisit it periodically. Lastly, make a decision as to when and how you want it distributed, seriously considering the very meaningful option of sharing it during your lifetime.

You're done. Good work. Congratulations.